Writing Your Own Book? Let's Talk

Writing Your Own Book? Let's Talk

Steve Garner

Better than Bonkers

CONTENTS

First Printing, 2023

Published by Better than Bonkers
A Bald and Bonkers Network LLC Imprint

ISBN: 979-8-8690-5353-4
EISBN: 979-8-8690-5354-1

Introduction

So, you've entertained the thought of writing a book to elevate your business and position yourself as an authority in your field. It's a fantastic idea, but let's face it – writing a book can be a challenging endeavor, even for seasoned wordsmiths. In this expansive guide, we'll delve into a myriad of strategies that can expedite the process, allowing you to have your book completed within the next month, whether you decide to take up the pen yourself or enlist the expertise of another writer.

The notion that you can own the complete copyright to a book without actually doing the writing might seem too good to be true, but there's a fascinating legal twist that makes it possible. By hiring a writer, you can bring your vision to life, and once the ink is dry, the copyright is yours. It's a legitimate and efficient option that's well worth considering, especially if the blank page seems like an insurmountable hurdle.

Selecting a captivating and relevant topic is a pivotal first step. Fortunately, this process is more straightforward than you might think. People are constantly scouring the internet for information, providing a treasure trove of inspiration for your next literary venture. By the time you finish this guide, you'll feel empowered to choose a topic that resonates with your audience or even pluck one directly from the pages of this guide itself – a win-win scenario for any aspiring author.

Discovering that "Aha moment" involves keen observation of your surroundings. Identify your interests, reflect on problems you or those around you have recently solved, and consider the myriad of issues others are grappling with. Any problem that has been resolved in your world could serve as an excellent subject for your book. So, grab a pen and start brainstorming a list of both solved and unsolved problems. The latter, in particular, can be gold mines for unique and sought-after book topics. Remember, you don't need to be the problem-solving expert; you just need an intriguing topic that captivates your audience.

Harnessing the power of the internet is a vital aspect of your book-writing journey. Platforms like Google, Yahoo!, and others can serve as invaluable tools to identify current trends and interests. Delving into bestseller lists on prominent platforms such as Amazon provides a pulse on what subjects are actively capturing the attention of readers.

A quick virtual visit to www.amazon.com and a glance at the "Top Sellers" tab revealed a wealth of popular nonfiction books. This not only re-affirmed the enduring appeal of best-selling fiction but also underscored the robust demand for nonfiction topics related to self-improvement and wealth creation. It's a noteworthy revelation that the nonfiction market offers a clear and direct path to book profits, making it an enticing prospect for aspiring authors.

Perhaps one of the most empowering realizations on your journey to authorship is that ideas are not copyrighted. This means that any idea you stumble upon, whether within the pages of a book, on the vast expanses of the internet, or elsewhere, is fair game for your creative endeavors. While copyright law protects the specific expression of ideas, it doesn't stifle your ability to explore a familiar subject with a unique voice. So, feel free to traverse the bestseller lists for inspiration, ensuring that your book covers a well-loved topic but with your distinct perspective.

In essence, this guide is designed to be your literary compass, pointing you toward the shores of authorship success. Whether you choose to embrace the solitude of writing or delegate the task to a capable wordsmith, the potential for success is within your grasp as you navigate the exciting and dynamic world of publishing. So, embark on this transformative journey armed with insights, strategies, and the unwavering confidence to make your mark in the literary landscape. The blank page awaits, and with the right approach, your book could be the next literary sensation that captivates minds and hearts alike.

Identifying Profitable Book Topics

The literary landscape is teeming with potential gold mines, and one of the richest veins lies within the realm of nonfiction books tailored for avid hobbyists. These individuals, passionate about their interests, present a unique opportunity for aspiring authors to transform their enthusiasm into financial gain. The key to success is to align your book with what hobbyists want, not necessarily what they need, as immediate profit often stems from catering to their fervor.

To identify these niche groups and hobbyist

communities, scour the web for terms like "popular hobbies," "enthusiasts," or "what America is buying." Alternatively, delve into forums and discussion groups dedicated to specific hobbies. Platforms like Yahoo! Groups provide a wealth of information, allowing you to tap into discussions, uncover popular topics, and discern what enthusiasts are actively seeking.

For instance, exploring the "Games" category on Yahoo! Groups unveils the extensive and passionate subcultures within hobbies like role-playing games, video games, and more. By immersing yourself in these forums, you gain insights into what these hobbyists are purchasing, providing you with a blueprint for creating a book that caters to their current interests and needs.

But the quest for book topics doesn't end with hobbyists alone. The ever-expanding internet offers a plethora of avenues for research. Utilize search engines like Google or Yahoo! to identify popular nonfiction books on platforms like Amazon and the New York Times bestseller list. Analyzing these trends reveals what subjects are actively captivating readers' attention, guiding you toward potentially lucrative book topics.

Venturing into the realm of how-to books adds another dimension to your literary pursuits. The market for instructional manuals, advice, and encouragement is insatiable, making how-to books a versatile and profitable genre. Whether you're delving into hobbies, DIY projects, or life enrichment, there's virtually no limit to the marketability of how-to books.

Consider aligning your book with established series like the "Dummies" books or "The Everything" series. These series have successfully capitalized on the widespread hunger for how-to information, catering to readers who seek straightforward guidance without unnecessary tangential discussions.

Moreover, the rise of ebooks allows for more targeted and specific content. Instead of crafting a universal guide, narrow down your focus to niche readerships. For instance, if you decide to write about fishing, you can create separate ebooks on specific aspects like "How to Catch Freshwater Trout," "How to Tie Your Own Flies," or "How to Plan a Successful Deep Sea Fishing Trip."

The insatiable appetite for staying youthful provides a fertile ground for book topics. Whether it's dropping years and pounds in days or exploring natural remedies, readers are eager for solutions to the age-old quest for eternal youth. Titles like "Drop ten years and ten pounds in ten days" or "100 ways to look younger" resonate with a market eager to defy the aging process.

Health, an evergreen concern for individuals of all ages, offers a vast array of potential book topics. From disease prevention and natural remedies to diet and general well-being, health-related books cater to a broad and enduring readership. Tackling subjects like coping with specific illnesses or exploring holistic health approaches can meet the needs of an audience hungry for valuable insights.

Travel, intertwined with various subjects, opens up diverse opportunities for book topics. Readers are eager for customized travel guides that align with their hobbies, interests, and lifestyles. Crafting books on unique travel experiences, combining hobbies with travel, or providing insider tips on specific destinations can tap into this wanderlust-driven market.

Money, being a perennial concern, invites authors to explore a plethora of how-to book topics. Whether it's frugal living, smart investments, or innovative financial strategies, there's always room for more books on money matters. Titles like "How to feed your family on less than $40 a week" or "How to be richer than your parents" resonate with readers seeking financial wisdom.

Self-help and life enrichment books are experiencing a surge in popularity, reflecting a societal desire for personal growth and fulfillment. Covering topics like finding peace with the past, cultivating creativity, or achieving true love provides authors with ample opportunities to contribute meaningful content to an eager audience.

Aspiring authors can further expand their literary horizons by tapping into trending topics. Exploring subjects like the latest electronics, home improvement, identity theft prevention, safety measures, or even pet care can cater to specific niches and address contemporary concerns.

For a market segment that dominates the internet, targeting topics of special interest to women presents a strategic opportunity. Addressing beauty, health, decorating, emotional support, and life enrichment with titles that resonate with female readers ensures a favorable reception in this influential demographic.

Lastly, the evergreen topic of sex remains a potent genre, with the internet providing a discreet and accessible avenue for interested readers. Whether exploring erotica or providing advice on relationships, there's an audience eager for content that navigates the nuances of human intimacy.

In conclusion, as you embark on your literary journey, consider these diverse and lucrative avenues for book topics. Whether catering to hobbyists, delving into how-to guides, or exploring timeless subjects like health and travel, the literary landscape is rich with opportunities for aspiring authors to strike gold with their words.

2

Navigating the Landscape

In the expansive realm of literary endeavors, the quest to bring forth your creative vision often involves a crucial step—securing the services of a writer for your book. This pivotal journey frequently leads to the realm of ghostwriters, individuals who, with mutual consent, pen works under someone else's name. This symbiotic collaboration allows individuals, ranging from celebrities seeking polished autobiographies to renowned authors optimizing their brand, to seamlessly translate their ideas into captivating narratives.

The practice of ghostwriting has evolved over time, extending its reach beyond individual books to encompass entire series. Some notable examples include the Hardy Boys series, where the elusive Franklin W. Dixon serves as the fictional cover author, and numerous romance novel series crafted by commissioned writers under a single authorial guise. In today's digital age, ghostwriters seamlessly transition to crafting books for the vast expanse of the Internet, offering a unique blend of creativity and expertise to those seeking literary excellence.

Unveiling the Talents of Ghostwriters

Beyond the mere act of writing, engaging a ghostwriter is a collaborative endeavor that ensures you, as the originator of the idea, remain the credited author. You provide guidance and direction to the ghostwriter, ensuring that the written material aligns with your vision. Moreover, this collaborative venture provides the option of maintaining anonymity through the adoption of a pen name, adding an extra layer of creativity to the process.

Ghostwriters excel at a myriad of tasks, extending beyond the act of writing itself. They possess the capability to conduct thorough research, transforming information into organized sections and crafting engaging, reader-friendly paragraphs. Additionally, ghostwriters can interview individuals identified by you or sourced by them to enrich the content of the book.

A skilled ghostwriter has the knack for discerning book-worthy material, keeping the narrative focused on the agreed-upon topic. The art lies in seamlessly incorporating intriguing elements that captivate readers, all while delivering the promised information highlighted in the title and table of contents.

Navigating the Writing Process

Ghostwriters bring versatility to the table by not only composing content but also aiding in the conceptualization phase. They can review your rough notes, propose compelling titles, and outline a table of contents. Starting from minimal input, a ghostwriter can weave a coherent narrative, ensuring that the final product aligns with your expectations.

For those who have attempted to embark on the challenging journey of writing a book independently, a ghostwriter can salvage existing drafts. Whether refining content, conducting necessary research, adding new sections, or enhancing grammar, a ghostwriter can elevate your manuscript to a sellable standard.

Crafting the Perfect Composition

One of the unique advantages of engaging a ghostwriter is their ability to adapt to your preferences. They can tailor the writing style, language, and perspective to suit the specific requirements of your book. Whether opting for a first-person narrative akin to this text or adopting a third-person perspective, ghostwriters are adept at accommodating your stylistic choices.

Formatting and Final Touches

Beyond the written content, ghostwriters offer expertise in formatting. They can customize the layout, font, and page dimensions according to your preferences. The flexibility extends to providing electronic files in formats such as MS Word, WordPerfect, Adobe Acrobat, Internet HTML, or others, based on your requirements.

Furthermore, ghostwriters are known for their efficiency, with the ability to deliver completed projects in a relatively short timeframe. While miracles aren't guaranteed, some ghostwriters can produce a book within 30 days, accommodating tight schedules. This expeditious approach is particularly advantageous for those who require prompt delivery.

Seamless Collaboration in the Digital Era

Engaging a ghostwriter is a streamlined process that allows you to delegate the task while maintaining control over the creative direction. Communication typically occurs through email, keeping the interaction efficient and well-documented. While other communication methods, such as phone calls or regular mail, are possible, the virtual nature of the collaboration aligns with the often tight schedules and lower budgets associated with ghostwritten books.

Unlocking the Value of Ghostwriters

Time is a precious commodity, and the decision to engage a ghostwriter becomes an investment in efficiency. By outsourcing the writing process, you free up valuable time to focus on other aspects of your project, be it marketing, ideation, or personal pursuits. The advantages lie in the accessibility, legality, and availability of writers willing to provide their services.

Peering into the Realm of Ghostwriters

Discovering a suitable ghostwriter can be approached through various avenues. The conventional method involves scouring writing or authoring organizations worldwide, interviewing writers until finding a suitable match. Alternatively, the digital age offers a more convenient route—exploring online platforms where ghostwriters congregate, responding to project ads. Notable platforms include Elance and Guru, which boast substantial traffic and a multitude of available ghostwriters.

A third avenue involves direct contact with ghostwriting companies, providing a more curated selection of experienced writers. When navigating these options, opting for platforms with high ghostwriter traffic is recommended for a more streamlined and efficient hiring process.

In the upcoming discussion, we will delve into

the specifics of locating available ebook ghostwriters and touch upon considerations related to pricing. As we embark on this journey, the aim is to equip you with the knowledge to make informed decisions and collaborate effectively with the right ghostwriter for your literary aspirations. Through this exploration, we aim to unravel the layers of the writing process, revealing the myriad facets that contribute to the creation of literary masterpieces.

Exploring the Vast Landscape of Ghostwriters for Your Book

Embarking on the exciting journey of bringing your book to life often involves the invaluable assistance of ghostwriters. These skilled individuals, discreetly working behind the scenes, can transform your ideas into captivating narratives. The digital age has paved the way for efficient collaboration with ghostwriters, offering a myriad of options to find the perfect match for your literary aspirations.

The two prominent online freelancer platforms where ghostwriters thrive, namely Elance and Guru, operate in similar fashions. You initiate the process by posting an ad, inviting responses from prospective ghostwriters. The vast catalogs of freelancers on these platforms encompass various services, and navigating to the realm of ebook projects and ghostwriting requires a bit of exploration. However, once you familiarize yourself with the platforms, the process becomes seamless.

To access the ghostwriting services on Elance, visit www.elance.com and navigate to the "Marketplace" section. Click on "Writing & Translation" from the menu on the left-hand side, and continue exploring until you locate the ebook projects database. Adding this URL to your browser's favorites can streamline future visits.

It's important to note that on Elance, writers are referred to as "service providers." This term distinguishes them from internet service providers or the Elance website's services themselves. On Guru, writers go by the title of "registered professionals."

Browsing through existing ads in Elance's writing marketplace provides valuable insights into how others find ghostwriters and the typical compensation for projects. While posting ads is free for clients, ghostwriters pay to review these ads, ensuring a fair and transparent process. Subscribing to Elance is necessary for posting ads, providing necessary information to establish trust between parties.

Upon posting your ad, the magic begins. Writers interested in your project submit online bids, engaging in a friendly competition to secure your business. The bids may include offers to write your book at a lower cost or a faster turnaround time than stated in your ad. Each responder furnishes background information, including links to their Elance history, portfolio, and client ratings.

Selecting the right ghostwriter involves careful consideration of the provided information, similar to evaluating vendors on eBay. This detailed process ensures you make an informed decision based on the writer's track record, client satisfaction, and experience.

Elance facilitates the creation of agreements between you and the chosen writer, streamlining payment through the platform. While a finder's fee is deducted from the payment, it ensures a secure and trustworthy transaction. Guru operates similarly, with fees varying based on subscription levels and services offered.

While the database platforms provide an efficient and competitive marketplace, there are alternative routes to finding ghostwriters. Directly contacting individual ghostwriters or exploring writing organizations can offer a more personalized approach. However, this method requires diligent research and reference checks to ensure the writer aligns with your vision.

Ebook reselling, another option discussed, allows you to purchase pre-written ebooks for resale. However, this approach comes with its drawbacks, including the lack of uniqueness and potential conflicts arising from shared resale rights. Ghostwriting, on the other hand, grants you exclusive ownership and control over your distinct literary creation.

In the dynamic landscape of ghostwriting, setting clear expectations in your project ad is crucial. Including a concise project description, maximum budget, bid closure date, and deadline for the ghostwriter ensures a smooth and focused collaboration. Exploring other ads on the platforms can serve as a template, providing valuable insights into structuring your own ad.

Ultimately, the path you choose depends on your preferences, but ghostwriting stands out as a personalized and creative way to bring your book to life. With careful consideration, effective communication, and a thorough understanding of the process, you'll find the perfect ghostwriter to turn your literary dreams into reality.

Discovering Your Ideal Writer

Exciting News! Following the placement of your initial advertisement, in a matter of days, if not minutes, you are likely to find multiple free-lancers eagerly responding, expressing their interest in ghostwriting your book. Should you choose to explore ghostwriting services beyond freelance platforms, the responses and enthusiasm for your project are likely to pour in promptly.

At this juncture, the delightful challenge arises as you must select the writer who aligns best with your vision. While opting for the lowest bid may be tempting, investing a few additional minutes in the selection process could save you from potential heartache. Your goal is to identify a writer who not only offers a competitive price but also assures a commendable job, timely delivery, and a cooperative working relationship.

Begin by meticulously examining the details provided by each bidder in response to your ad. Look for writers with verified credentials and positive client reviews on platforms like Elance or Guru. Verified credentials are particularly valuable, as they are officially confirmed by the platform through transcripts or diplomas.

Review client ratings on Elance or Guru, as they offer insights into the satisfaction levels of previous clients. While not all clients may provide feedback, those who do offer valuable perspectives on the working relationship and the quality of the final product.

For ghostwriting services obtained through platforms or individual writers, scrutinize the references provided by the writer. Don't merely glance at the length of the reference list; delve deeper by obtaining contact information and reaching out to these references. Hearing firsthand about a writer's performance is invaluable in making an informed decision.

Given the confidential nature of ghostwriting, writers may not share specific works but can provide writing samples they created for personal benefit or under their name. Request at least one or two writing samples to gauge the writer's style, language command, and attention to detail.

In addition to ratings, references, and writing samples, consider the writer's language proficiency. It is advisable to inquire about fluency, and even request a native speaker if necessary. Effectively communicating with your writer is crucial for the success of your book.

While concise responses to ads are common, be cautious of glaring errors in a writer's reply. Attention to detail is paramount, and significant errors may indicate a lack of suitability for your project.

Beware of writers making extravagant claims, such as promising a 100-page book in a matter of days. Quality writing, especially for in-depth coverage or research, requires time and expertise. Avoid wasting time on unrealistic offers.

Amid the variety of potential writers, exercise caution against selecting the lowest or highest bids. Evaluate each candidate based on a comprehensive assessment of their credentials, references, samples, and ratings.

Once satisfied with your chosen writer, it's essential to establish a written agreement. Utilize contracts provided by freelancing platforms or carefully negotiate and review contracts from individual ghostwriting sites with the assistance of legal counsel if necessary.

Preparation for Future Projects:

Recognize that a great ghostwriter goes beyond delivering a good product; fostering a trust-based, long-term working relationship is invaluable. Pay reasonable rates, acknowledge your writer's efforts, and provide constructive feedback. Repeat business and positive referrals are indicators of a good working relationship.

When searching for a book cover art designer, explore local art organizations or conduct an internet search using relevant keywords. Alternatively, observe well-marketed ebooks and reach out to webmasters for recommendations on cover designers.

Choosing a designer involves evaluating their fees, responsiveness, examples of previous work, satisfaction guarantees, turnaround times, revision policies, and additional services they may offer. Investing time in finding a reliable cover designer pays off when embarking on multiple ebook projects.

> Tip: Inquire about web services fees when discussing ebook cover art, as having a designer who can align your cover design with your marketing web page is advantageous. A skilled artist can provide titles, banners, buttons, and other related web page elements.

Diving Deeper into the Elements of an Exceptional Book Cover

Embarking on the creative journey of crafting a book cover involves entrusting a designer with the pivotal task of visually representing your literary creation. While relinquishing some control, you can fortify your collaboration by posing thoughtful questions and offering insightful answers, ensuring that the final product aligns seamlessly with your vision.

Evaluating Standout Artwork:

The importance of ensuring that your artwork boldly stands out on your web page cannot be overstated. The last thing you want is for it to blend into the background or become a mere after-thought. Consider the various elements—color, texture, shape, exclamation points, or professional artwork—that can infuse your cover with the necessary pizzazz to capture the attention of potential readers. Simplicity, an art in itself, is often the key. Delve into the designs of your chosen artist, seeking that distinctive "standout" factor that resonates with your book's essence.

Analyzing the Prominence of the Title:

A clutter-free cover is crucial, and your title should be at the forefront, making a lasting impression. Assess the layout to ensure that a quick scroll through web pages leaves an indelible mark of your book's title. If, after a passing glance, the title fails to etch itself into your memory, it might be time for a rejuvenating touch-up.

Navigating the Color Palette:

The strategic use of color plays a pivotal role in the visual appeal of your cover. Opt for a limited palette—four colors or fewer—to avoid overwhelming your audience. Psychologically appealing colors such as red, blue, or yellow, combined with black and white, can be a potent combination. Simplicity remains key, steering clear of excessive colors or textures that might detract from the professionalism of your cover. Experiment with different combinations to find the one that resonates best with your book's theme.

Ensuring Text Readability:

The legibility of text on your cover is paramount. Choose fonts that are familiar and easy to read, steering away from intricate styles that might pose challenges for potential buyers. Clarity in communication is crucial, and the chosen font should facilitate quick and effortless comprehension. The readability of your cover text is an aspect that should not be compromised.

Crafting a Three-Dimensional Appearance:

In the digital realm, the allure of a physical book is not lost. Ensure that your cover boasts a three-dimensional appearance, complete with a spine and the illusion of internal pages. A mere flat representation of the front cover is insufficient for a web audience seeking a tangible connection to the literary world. Embrace the reality that readers, despite their technological savvy, are drawn to online artwork that evokes the cherished feel of a physical book.

Extending Your Research Horizon:

As you embark on the extensive journey of researching and crafting your book, a treasure trove of web resources and links awaits your exploration. Each item listed in this section has been meticulously curated based on research and firsthand experience. Whether previously discussed or included for informational purposes, these resources offer valuable insights into site layouts and vendor availability.

It's essential to clarify that the recommendations made are entirely impartial, devoid of any affiliations with the listed companies or individuals. The objective is to empower readers with information, encouraging them to explore references and leverage additional services they may encounter on their creative journey.

Unveiling Ebook Ghostwriters:

- [Elance](www.elance.com): As extensively discussed before, this platform houses a substantial database of ghostwriters eager to contribute their expertise to your literary endeavors.

- [Guru](www.guru.com): Positioned as a larger counterpart to Elance, Guru boasts an expansive database of ghostwriters, providing you with an array of options to explore and select from.

Summing Up the Journey:

The odyssey of discovering how to bring your book to fruition, even without personally crafting each word, has undoubtedly been a rewarding experience. Outsourcing aspects of your book creation involves a financial investment, but the dividends in terms of time saved and potential returns on your investment are significant. Your initial challenge of conceptualizing your book's theme becomes the focal point, with the remaining facets open to outsourcing or rapid execution by following the comprehensive guidance provided in this book.

The allure of becoming a part of the esteemed community of authors is palpable, and your eagerness to navigate the intricate process is commendable. While my personal journey included stumbling and learning from mistakes, your path is poised to be more seamless. Embrace the learning process, navigate occasional bumps with resilience, and, should challenges arise, dust off and rejoin the exhilarating game of book creation. The journey ahead promises growth, creativity, and the fulfillment of bringing your literary vision to life.

Bonus Articles

So, You Aspire to Embark on the Journey of Writing a Book?

Congratulations on completing your manuscript! If you find yourself standing at the threshold of becoming a published author, especially for the first time, you might be grappling with uncertainties about the next steps. Fret not, for the following comprehensive guide unveils a series of crucial steps you should consider to navigate the intricate path of book publication successfully.

Navigating the Publisher Landscape:
The initial step involves immersing yourself in the world of publishers. Beyond merely identifying where to submit your manuscript and the appropriate addressee, delve into understanding the intricacies of

the potential publisher. Questions abound: What thematic preferences do they harbor? Does your book align with their interests? Are there specific formatting rules and restrictions you must adhere to? Do they exclusively consider agented submissions? Having answers to these questions is pivotal for a successful submission.

Scouring for Suitable Publishers:

The quest to find the perfect publisher for your manuscript opens up a realm of diverse options. Survey your personal book collection, visit your local library, or peruse the shelves of nearby bookstores. Identify the publishers behind books that resonate with your genre. Conduct a meticulous internet search using the names of these publishers, and explore the writer's guidelines on their websites. Broader searches, such as "book publishers," can also unveil potential matches. Don't overlook printed resources like the acclaimed Writer's Market books, which offer a wealth of information.

Unraveling Rules and Restrictions:
Understanding the nuanced guidelines and constraints set by publishing companies is paramount. In cases where this information eludes online or printed sources, exercise your best judgment. Ensure that your manuscript is not only well-written but also impeccably formatted and presented. Alongside your manuscript, incorporate a concise cover letter and a compelling book proposal. While some authors choose to amalgamate these documents, caution must be exercised to maintain clarity and brevity.

Harnessing Professional Assistance:
Considering the services of a professional literary agent and editor can elevate the quality and marketability of your manuscript. Despite the associated costs, the benefits often outweigh the expenses. A fresh set of professional eyes is invaluable for catching errors that may have eluded even the most meticulous self-proofreading. Literary agents, in particular, offer a strategic advantage, especially when targeting publishers

that exclusively consider agented submissions. Their expertise can open doors that might otherwise remain closed.

Crafting Appropriate Follow-Ups:
After submitting your manuscript, the waiting game begins. While it's acceptable to initiate follow-ups, exercising prudence is crucial. Publishers typically outline the expected response time on their websites, typically ranging from two to four months. Should this timeframe elapse without a response, consider a courteous inquiry via phone or letter. However, refrain from reaching out before the estimated response time to safeguard your professional image.

Embracing Resilience in the Face of Rejections:
As you navigate the intricate journey towards publication, it's essential to recognize rejection as an integral part of the process. Rejection letters are commonplace, but they should never deter your passion and commitment. Perseverance in the face of

rejection is a testament to your dedication to seeing your literary creation come to life.

In conclusion, by meticulously considering the aforementioned points, you pave the way for the potential realization of your dream to see your book in print. It's important to remember that rejection is not a roadblock but rather a stepping stone on the path to success. So, take heart, stay resilient, and let the world witness the fruition of your literary endeavors.

Embarking on the Journey of Writing: Challenges and Strategies

Have you ever contemplated writing a book, perhaps with the lofty aspiration of seeing it published? If you're a budding author, the prospect of undertaking this monumental task might seem daunting. The question often arises: What's the easiest route to take? After all, minimizing unnecessary workload is a universal desire among writers. Many find themselves pondering which genre or type of book stands a better chance of being published effortlessly.

The reality is that determining which books are easier to get published isn't a straightforward quest. In truth, the path to publishing, whether it involves a children's book or a romantic novel, is fraught with challenges. It demands substantial time, effort, determination, and thorough research. However, fret not, for there are numerous steps you can embrace to navigate this intricate journey with relative ease.

To commence this literary journey, it's crucial to select a genre, topic, or theme that resonates with your passion. This is particularly true for instructional books or informative guides. While writing should be approached as a professional endeavor, it should never feel burdensome. Hence, choosing a subject that genuinely interests you and evokes passion is paramount. For instance, if you're a parent, delving into children's literature could be a rewarding choice. Similarly, if you're enamored with science fiction, penning a novel in that genre might be your calling.

Opting for a genre that aligns with your interests not only simplifies the writing process but also enhances your chances of getting published. Genuine passion often translates into superior content, encouraging meticulous proofreading and editing—qualities that might set you apart from authors solely motivated by financial gains.

Regardless of the genre you choose, conducting preliminary research is indispensable. While writing about a topic close to your heart is crucial, understanding publishers' preferences is equally vital. Did you know, for instance, that mysteries are in high demand for chapter books and early adult novels? Uncovering such insights can be achieved through research, utilizing resources like the Writer's Market books or conducting online searches.

Crafting a book centered on a story or topic that aligns with your passion and coincides with publishers' interests substantially elevates your chances of securing a publishing deal. It's imperative to acknowledge the fluidity and ease that arises when you write about something you are deeply passionate about and align it with market demand.

As a gentle reminder, there isn't a one-size-fits-all answer to the question of which type of book is easier to get published. Publishers universally share the common goal of putting forth a marketable book, which leads to stringent standards across genres. Every genre demands commitment, creativity, and an understanding of the market dynamics to overcome the challenges inherent in the publishing process.

In conclusion, as you embark on the arduous yet rewarding journey of writing, remember that the challenges are inherent, but so are the strategies for overcoming them.

Passion, coupled with strategic research, can pave the way for your literary creation to find its rightful place in the world of published works. So, fear not, fellow writer, and let your words flow freely onto the pages of your manuscript.

Navigating the Path to Publication: Key Considerations for Authors

Congratulations on completing your manuscript! The journey of writing a book is undoubtedly a significant accomplishment, and the prospect of seeing it published is both thrilling and rewarding. As you contemplate sending your manuscript to potential publishers, it's crucial to embark on this next phase with knowledge and caution. Understanding the intricacies of the publishing process is vital to ensure you make informed decisions and avoid potential pitfalls that could compromise your efforts.

A fundamental aspect to bear in mind

when seeking to publish your book is that different publishers have specific preferences and criteria. The literary landscape is diverse, with publishers catering to various genres and themes. For instance, within the realm of children's books, one publisher might be seeking science-fiction for young adults, while another is interested in nature-inspired picture books. Before submitting your manuscript, it's imperative to research each publisher's specific requirements to align your work with their current needs. This strategic approach helps you avoid investing time and resources in submitting to publishers who may not be a suitable fit for your book at the given time.

Delving into the details of a publisher's guidelines is equally essential. Each publisher has distinct submission protocols, whether they require full manuscripts, sample chapters, or query letters. Adhering to these guidelines is critical, as failure to do so can significantly diminish your chances of having your book accepted. Resources such as the Writer's Market books and online platforms provide valuable insights into what publishers expect from aspiring authors.

Payment considerations are another crucial aspect that demands careful examination before accepting an offer from a publisher. Not all publishers offer the same compensation, and understanding the nuances of payment structures is vital. While the excitement of receiving an offer may be overwhelming, it's essential not to lose sight of your ultimate goal – maximizing your earnings. Payment methods, including flat rate payments, advance payments, and royalty payments, are common in the publishing industry.

When evaluating advance payments, it's imperative to scrutinize the long-term implications. Some publishers may present advance payments enticingly but may not offer favorable terms in the overall context. As a first-time author, the allure of advance payments might be strong, but a thorough understanding of the agreement's implications is crucial.

Royalty payments require meticulous attention to detail. Ensure that all terms are clearly outlined in the contract, including the percentage of sales you will receive, the frequency of royalty calculations (quarterly or annually), and the timeline for payment after each period. Having these details in writing provides transparency and protects your interests as an author.

The points highlighted above are just a glimpse into the myriad considerations you should factor in before accepting an offer from a book publisher. Regardless of your book's genre or the publisher you engage with, it's essential to scrutinize and fully comprehend the terms outlined in the contract. Do not hesitate to ask questions and seek clarification on any aspects that may be unclear. Reputable publishers will appreciate your diligence and be willing to address your concerns. Remember, this journey is not just about getting your book published; it's about ensuring that the terms are fair, transparent, and conducive to a successful and rewarding author-publisher relationship.

Embarking on the Journey of Publishing: A Comprehensive Exploration of the Steps

Dreaming of becoming a published writer is a commendable goal, but the path to seeing your book in print can be intricate and challenging. If you're ready to take the plunge into the world of publishing, it's essential to understand the crucial steps that will guide you through this exciting but often daunting process. Let's delve into the key stages, unraveling the intricacies of getting your book published.

1. The Genesis: Writing Your Book
The journey begins with the creation of your literary masterpiece. But, hold on—

don't rush into the writing phase without strategic forethought. Investigate popular genres and discover what types of books are currently sought after by publishers. Avoid common pitfalls, such as assuming that writing a children's book is an easier route to success. While it may be your passion, it's crucial to recognize that children's books, like any other genre, demand dedication and skill.

2. The Polishing Phase: Proofreading and Editing

Once your book is written or nearing completion, the next step is a meticulous proofreading process. This isn't a one-and-done affair; triple-check for errors and seek input from trusted friends or relatives. Consider providing a few chapters to review for longer books. If professional editing isn't in your budget, leveraging the fresh perspective of others can catch overlooked mistakes and refine your manuscript.

3. The Crossroads: Literary Agents or DIY Approach

Now, you stand at a crucial crossroads—deciding whether to enlist the services of a literary agent or take the do-it-yourself route. For adult books, many renowned publishers prefer authors with literary representation. Although not mandatory, having a literary agent may open doors to more opportunities. Explore reputable agents, scrutinize their fees, read client testimonials, and assess success rates before making this pivotal decision.

4. The DIY Route: Researching Book Publishers

Opting to navigate the publishing waters independently? Brace yourself for a deep dive into researching book publishers. Avoid costly mistakes by investing time in comprehensive research. Writer's guides like the esteemed Writer's Market or online resources can provide invaluable information. Learn about publishers' guidelines, submission windows, and any specific rules or restrictions they may have.

5. The Art of Persistence: Facing Rejections

Rejections are part of the publishing journey, especially for unpublished authors. Rarely does lightning strike on the first attempt. Maintain resilience, and don't let rejection letters deter you. Experiment with different publishers, and if the rejections pile up, consider revisiting your book. Are there tweaks to the storyline or layout that could enhance your chances? The key is to persist and adapt.

6. The Ongoing Odyssey: Continuous Improvement

Getting a book published is not a one-and-done process. Continuous improvement is the name of the game. Stay informed about evolving publishing trends, revisit your manuscript, and be open to refinement. Seek feedback, experiment with different approaches, and stay dedicated to honing your craft.

In conclusion, the steps outlined above are a foundational guide to the intricate process of getting a book published. While these steps are by no means exhaustive, they provide a solid starting point for aspiring authors. Remember, research is your ally, persistence is your strength, and continuous improvement is your companion on this exhilarating journey toward becoming a published writer. So, pen those thoughts, polish your prose, and embark on the adventure of bringing your book to the hands of eager readers.

Exploring the Realm of Self-Publishing: Is it the Right Path for You?

For many aspiring authors, the dream of seeing their work in print can be a daunting journey, especially when faced with rejection letters from traditional publishing houses. However, in the digital age, a viable alternative has emerged – self-publishing. The question arises: should you take the leap and self-publish your own book? Let's delve into the nuances of this alternative and explore the signs that may point you towards this path.

Understanding Self-Publishing

Before we explore whether self-publishing is the right fit, it's crucial to grasp the essence of this approach. Self-publishing entails the author taking charge of the entire process, from writing and editing to finding a printer and marketing the book. Authors often sell their self-published works through their websites or approach various retailers.

Signs That Self-Publishing Might Be Your Best Option

Sign #1 – You Have Received Multiple Rejection Letters

Rejections are a common facet of the traditional publishing process. Many successful authors faced numerous rejections before securing a deal. If you find yourself accumulating rejection letters without success, consider it a rite of passage. Exhaust your traditional publishing options before contemplating self-publishing.

Sign #2 – Despite Rejection Letters, You Still Believe You Have a Good Book

Belief in your work is paramount. If, despite the rejections, you have unwavering confidence in the quality of your book, self-publishing might be a fitting avenue for you. Passion for your creation will drive the self-publishing journey.

Sign #3 – You Have a Book with Limited Readers

Not all books cater to a broad audience, and that's perfectly fine. If you've written a niche book, a how-to guide, or a specialized work likely to attract a limited readership, self-publishing becomes an attractive option. Traditional publishers might shy away from works with smaller target audiences.

Sign #4 – You Want to Retain the Largest Profit

Financial considerations play a pivotal role in the decision-making process. Self-published authors have the advantage of retaining a larger share of their profits since they don't contend with publisher fees. While self-publishing comes with its own set of costs, it's often more cost-effective compared to the traditional publishing model.

Navigating the Self-Publishing Landscape

While the allure of retaining creative control and maximizing profits is enticing, it's crucial to approach self-publishing with a realistic mindset. Proper marketing efforts are imperative for success, and authors should be prepared to invest time and resources in promoting their work.

Pros and Cons of Self-Publishing

As with any decision, there are pros and cons to self-publishing. The autonomy it offers and the potential for higher profits are appealing, but the onus of marketing and distribution falls squarely on the author's shoulders. Carefully weighing these factors against your goals and resources will help you make an informed decision.

In conclusion, self-publishing is a viable and empowering option for authors who find traditional publishing avenues challenging. If you possess a deep belief in your work, have a niche audience, and are willing to navigate the complexities of marketing, self-publishing may open new doors for your literary aspirations. Remember, each writer's journey is unique, and the path to success may take various forms – self-publishing being one of them.

Navigating the Self-Publishing Journey: Avoiding Common Pitfalls

Embarking on the self-publishing route is an empowering choice for authors who seek independence and control over their work. If you have faced rejection letters from traditional publishing companies but believe in the marketability of your book, self-publishing may be the right avenue for you. However, in the realm of self-publishing, it's crucial to tread carefully and steer clear of potential pitfalls that could tarnish your journey. Let's explore some common self-publishing mistakes and how to avoid them.

1. Signing Unnecessary Contracts

A key advantage of self-publishing is the freedom it offers, and you should not find yourself entangled in unnecessary contracts. When seeking a printing company to turn your manuscript into a book, avoid signing contracts that demand more than the agreed-upon fee. If a contract surfaces, be wary, as this could indicate dealings with a vanity publisher rather than a straightforward printing service.

2. Beware of Recommendations with Hidden Agendas

While seeking assistance for your self-published book, exercise caution when receiving recommendations. If someone suggests a designer or service, consider the possibility of hidden motives. Some recommendations might be fueled by financial incentives, where the recommender earns a percentage of each sale as an affiliate. Validate the credibility of any suggested service independently.

3. Guarding Your Completed Work

If you decide to hire professionals like designers or editors, be cautious about handing over your completed work without due diligence. A reputable designer only needs an outline or your expectations, not the entire manuscript. Should anyone request your complete work without a valid reason, it raises red flags, and you should proceed with caution.

4. *Vigilance in Hiring Professional Editors*

When hiring a professional editor, conduct thorough research to ensure their legitimacy and trustworthiness. Editors play a crucial role in refining your work, but entrusting them with your intellectual property demands caution. Beware of editors who provide minimal feedback and then present a bill, as this might indicate a lack of genuine engagement with your manuscript.

5. *Separating Publishing and Marketing Services*

One downside of self-publishing is the responsibility of marketing falling on the author's shoulders. While seeking external assistance for marketing is common, it's essential to separate the entities handling publishing and marketing. Avoid companies that insist on both publishing and selling your book, as this could be indicative of a potential scam. Instead, consider hiring a dedicated marketing specialist to help establish your online presence or approach local retailers independently.

Conclusion: Navigating the Self-Publishing Landscape

Despite potential pitfalls and scams associated with self-publishing, it remains a valuable avenue for authors to bring their work to the public. By exercising caution, conducting thorough research, and making informed decisions, you can navigate the self-publishing landscape successfully. Remember, your judgment is your best ally in ensuring a positive and fulfilling self-publishing experience.

www.ingramcontent.com/pod-product-compliance
Lightning Source LLC
Chambersburg PA
CBHW061442160726
47995CB00003B/1002